365 WAYS TO KISS YOUR LOVE

A DAILY GUIDE TO CREATIVE KISSING

BY TOMIMA EDMARK

MJF BOOKS
NEW YORK

Published by MJF Books
Fine Communications
Two Lincoln Square
60 West 66th Street
New York, NY 10023

365 Ways to Kiss Your Love
Library of Congress Catalog Card Number 97-75443
ISBN 1-56731-235-7

Copyright © 1993 by The Summit Group.

This edition published by arrangement with The Summit Group.

Jacket Design by Cheryl Corbitt * Book Design by Rishi Seth

Manufactured in the United States of America on acid-free paper

MJF Books and the MJF colophon are trademarks of Fine Creative Media, Inc.

10   9   8   7   6   5   4   3   2

❤ TO MY LOVE ❤

_____

_____

_____

_____

_____

_____

PLACE A DROP
OF COLOGNE OR
YOUR LIP PRINT ABOVE

❤ INTRODUCTION ❤

It's curious to suddenly discover that you know more about kissing than anyone else. In interviews I'm always asked why I chose to be an expert on kissing. The truth is I didn't start out to be an expert on the subject.

The idea for my first book, *Kissing: Everything You Ever Wanted To Know*, came to me immediately after receiving a kiss during my college career. This kiss was particularly memorable because while my partner was proclaiming the kiss's greatness, I was examining my mouth for broken bridge work. How could two people have such different opinions about the same kiss?

This question sent me to the campus library the next day. I quickly discovered the subject of kissing had been grossly overlooked. There they were; thousands of books explaining in clinical detail every possible lovemaking configuration. Yet, there was nothing on that magical first step two people take on the path to intimacy. That wonderful simple kiss that can send tingles down your spine and leave you gaga in the afterglow hours after that person has left. This had to be changed. I spent the next 10 years researching and writing what is now my first book.

Having your first book published is a thrill for anyone. However, it was particularly sweet for me due to the fact I was diagnosed dyslexic while in high school. I had every intention of turning my notes over to someone else to write the book. I owe a debt of gratitude to Lucille Enix, an editor, who convinced me I could write it myself.

After the first book was published, I was persistently asked what my next book was going to be. Well here it is, what I believe to be the perfect follow-up. In the first book, I spelled out for you the tips and techniques, turn-ons and turn-offs, and advice from kissing experts. The next step is to find a partner and move from theory to practice. Consider this book a compilation of 365 kissing experiments.

My 365 kisses, as you'll soon find, are not written in gruesome detail. You will not read things such as "Open mouth, insert tongue and in a clockwise motion, beginning on the left incisor, move the tongue...." These kisses are situational. It is up to you to decide what kissing technique to use. This book is simply a catalyst to help you and your love create more kissing excitement.

Many of my ideas for the 365 kisses were conceived on airplanes, while running, or during everyday events such as showering. I always kept a notebook handy to write down all of my kissing ideas.

Kisses that are particularly memorable to me are the Kiss a L'Orange and the Bathroom Surprise Kiss. After running a 10K with friends, we all gathered together to eat orange quarters. Suddenly I thought of the orange kiss. The Bathroom Surprise Kiss came to me at the Plaza Hotel in New York around three in the morning. I couldn't sleep, so I was writing down ideas on my pad with the only pen I had at the time—a red-ink pen. I literally jumped out of bed and played with the idea until I mastered the correct technique. Of course, many kisses are from personal kissing experiences. But, then again, I don't kiss and tell.

Kissing is on the rise. With the threat of AIDS, people are becoming more monogamous. In my research, I found that the 50-and-over generation has the better kissers. This is no surprise when you remember that this generation courted. Kissing was all they could do, so they became very good at it. Let's bring back the art of kissing.

A final note. I am always asked about my name. Tomima is a family name on my mother's side. It's Scotch in origin (although

I'm three-quarters Swedish) and dates back to the 18th Century. It's pronounced like Aunt Jemima, but with a T. Now, turn the page, pucker up, and begin to discover all the different ways to kiss your Love.

♥ 1 ♥

ICE KISS

Celebrate the first day of winter with an ice
kiss. Put an ice cube in your mouth until your mouth becomes
cold. Remove the cube, track down your love and plant a
kiss that will send chills.

♥ 2 ♥

ELECTRIC KISS

The two of you shuffle your feet furiously on carpet. When
you both have an electric charge, lean over and slowly aim for
each other's lips. With your lips about one-half inch
apart, move in even slower until a spark jumps between the
two of you. Instantly after this happens, kiss one another...the
pleasure is the kiss right after the shock.

♥ 3 ♥

SLEEPING BAG KISS

On a beautiful cool night, you and your love crawl into a
sleeping bag outside. Cuddle and kiss.

• 4 •

REWARD KISS

Next time your love performs some disliked home
chore like cleaning the bathroom, mowing the lawn, or taking
out the garbage, show your appreciation by tucking a
candy *Kiss* in a strategic location.

• 5 •

HAPPY TRAIL KISS

Use stick-on notes to make a trail through your
house that leads to your lips. Put a lipstick print or lip symbol
on each note with an arrow pointing to the next note.
You, of course, are at the end of the trail with a stick-on note
over your lips that says, "Lift for Kiss."

• 6 •

KISSING IN THE RAIN

The next time it rains, grab an umbrella, rain
coats, and your love. Then go outside and kiss in the rain. If
the spirit moves you, remove the umbrella and kiss 'til
the two of you are soaked.

♥ 7 ♥

SUBSTITUTE KISSES

Prepare a small bag of candy kisses and slip it into
your love's purse, briefcase or lunchbox. *Attach a note that
reads: "Sorry I can't be there in person, but think of me and
do the following: Close you eyes and place the candy between your
lips. Drop the candy in your mouth and roll it on your tongue
until it melts." Suggestion: This is a great idea if your love is
leaving on a trip.*

♥ 8 ♥

TRACY & HEPBURN KISS

Make flash cards, and the two of you re-enact the following
kissing scene from *Woman of the Year (1942)*:

(Reclining face-to-face on a couch, woman on top.)
Sam: Something I've got to get off my chest.
Tess: I'm too heavy?
Sam: I love you.
Tess: Me, too.
Sam: Positive.
Tess: That's nice. Even when I'm sober?
Sam: Even when you're brilliant. (The two of you kiss.)

♥ 9 ♥

BALLOON KISSES

Cut out small red tissue lips and place them inside an opaque balloon filled with helium (any party goods store could do this for you). Tie the balloon to your love's chair at dinner. Dessert is a shower of kisses delivered by a sharp pin.

♥ 10 ♥

TOLL KISS

Next time you're driving your love somewhere, stop the car before crossing a bridge or going through a tunnel, and say the toll must be paid before you can go any further. Of course, the toll cost is one kiss.

♥ 11 ♥

MORSE CODE KISS

If you know Morse code, great. If not, this is a great way to learn. Find a Morse code chart. Using long and short kisses, spell out messages to your love and have him or her try to decipher them.

♥ 12 ♥

KISSING METER KISSES

We have parking meters, so why not kissing meters?
Turn a box into your own kissing meter and wear it around
your neck. Give your love kissing tokens to start your
kissing meter. Have an "expired" sign appear when you need
another kiss.

♥ 13 ♥

CASSETTE KISS

Make a cassette of kissing noises and place it in your
love's cassette player (*Walkman*, car or home) with a note
attached.

♥ 14 ♥

BREAKFAST-IN-BED KISSES

Slip out of bed early and prepare a special "Kissing"
breakfast to serve to your love in bed. Pick foods that you can
easily pick up and feed to your love. Kiss between bites.

• 15 •

BACKSTAIRS KISS
This kiss is to be done at a party or at a gathering
with your love. Steal away to a private location like behind a
door or tree, or on the backstairs and passionately
kiss each other. The risk of being discovered in the act is the
key element.

• 16 •

JACQUES COUSTEAU KISS
Wearing a diving mask and fins, simulate swimming
underwater. Snorkel across the room to your love and kiss
him or her.

• 17 •

EYE CHART KISS
Make an eye chart like the ones you see in a doctor's
office where the letters get progressively smaller. Have the
chart read, "If you can read this you are standing close enough
to kiss me." Now find your love and give an eye exam.

♥ 18 ♥

THYMELY KISS

Thyme, according to the Greeks, is the herb which
makes one irresistibly kissable. Prepare a meal for your love
using the herb. Moments after the first bite, rush to your love's
lips with a passionate kiss. Come up for air, announce the
Greeks were right, then rush back with another
passionate kiss.

♥ 19 ♥

GROCERY LIST KISSES

Turn your grocery list into a scorecard the next time
the two of you go shopping. The one who finds the item gets
credit toward one kiss. Kisses are collected either on
delivery to the grocery cart, or later at home. *Idea: Maximize
your kissing credits by discussing the kissing value of each item.
For instance, is a six-pack of Pepsi six kisses?*

♥ 20 ♥

BAD HABIT KISS

Offer to stop a bad habit if your love will pay you in kisses.
For instance, a kiss for each cigarette not smoked, putting the
toilet seat down, and/or every phone call kept under three
minutes is rewarded with a kiss.

♥ 21 ♥

CLOUD KISSES

Take your love to the backyard or out in a field; lie
down on a blanket, and together inspect cloud formations.
When both of you see the same thing, reward each
other with a kiss.

♥ 22 ♥

CHECK KISS

With your personal check, make a check out to your
love for 1,000 kisses. Tell your love he or she can cash it in
any time.

• 23 •

TOE KISS

Prepare a foot bath for your love at the end of a
long day. After the good soak, you towel dry his or her feet,
give a massage and seal each toe with a kiss.

• 24 •

CANDY HEART KISSES

Buy several boxes of little candy hearts that have
sayings on them. Pick out all the "Kiss Me" hearts and put
them in a heart-shaped box with the note, "Redeemable
anytime day or night."

• 25 •

RENDEZVOUS KISS

With a note or phone call, tell your love to meet you
at a certain place and time (e.g. park bench, street corner, ice
cream stand) for a present. When your love arrives, have
a bow stuck to your lips.

• 26 •

SHOWER KISS
Surprise your love with a kiss while he/she is showering.
Warning: Prepare to get wet.

• 27 •

RAPID-FIRE KISS
In rapid succession, plant 12 quick ones on your love's lips.

• 28 •

EXTRA LONG KISS
Passionately kiss your love for at least one minute
longer than usual. *Note: Do not attempt this kiss when either of you
is in a hurry.*

• 29 •

PINK PANTHER KISS
Humming the *Pink Panther* theme, prowl toward your
partner. On the high note, pounce and pucker. *Suggestion:
Wear only pink.*

• 30 •

THIRST-QUENCHER KISS

For no reason, stare at your love's mouth while licking
your lips as though dying of thirst. Inevitably, your love will
ask what you're doing. *Answer: "I want them! I have
to have them! I yearn to drink from them!" Then ask for a kiss to
quench your thirst.*

• 31 •

GREAT EXPECTATION KISS

Inform your love one morning that he or she will soon
receive a fabulous kiss. Later, call your love with a reminder.
When next you see your love, pull out the stops and
plant a long, hot, passionate kiss.

• 32 •

GOODBYE SURPRISE KISS

Send off your love in the morning with a quick kiss.
As your love turns to leave, pull him or her back for a second,
more passionate kiss.

• 33 •

RIDDLE KISS

Ask your love to solve the following riddle:

I am just two and two,
I am warm, I am cold,
I am lawful, unlawful
-A duty, a fault -
I am often sold dear,
Good for nothing when bought;
An extraordinary boon,
And a matter of course,
And yielding with pleasure
When taken by force.
(Riddle by William Cowper.)

If your love solves it, ask for a demonstration as proof. If he or she can't show the answer, of course, the answer is a kiss.

• 34 •

MANDATED KISS

Command your love to kiss you. Elaborate on the technique you expect (e.g. long and wet, or the way Rhett kissed Scarlett), and where and when you will get it.
Hint: A comical stance with hands on hips and feet slightly apart will help win your demand.

♥ 35 ♥

UNEXPECTED KISS
When the two of you are doing the usual (e.g. watching
TV, reading the paper, eating dinner), lean over and give your
love a sweet kiss on the cheek for no good reason and
whisper, "I love you."

♥ 36 ♥

POST OFFICE KISS
Notify your love you have personal mail to deliver. Pull
your love into the nearest dark closet; close the door and play
"Post Office." No instructions included.

♥ 37 ♥

KNOCK-KNOCK KISS
Stage the following knock-knock joke with your love:
You: "Knock-knock."
Love: "Who's there?"
You: "Kiss"
Love: "Kiss who?"
You: "Kiss who? Why me, of course."
You & Love: Kiss.

♥ 38 ♥

BEGGING KISS

That's right; on your knees with your hands clasped, plead for
any kiss your love is humbly willing to give you.

♥ 39 ♥

TOOTHBRUSH KISS

Brush your teeth together. When your love's mouth is
all sudsy, plant a big wet one on the lips. *Warning: Make sure
toothbrushes are out of the way.*

♥ 40 ♥

PALM KISS

Holding your love's face with your palms, smile and deliver a
sweet kiss to his or her lips.

♥ 41 ♥

10 KISSES

Inform your love that in honor of the 10th of the month, you
will kiss him or her 10 times today.

♥ 42 ♥

CAT KISS

Rub against your love's legs while meowing and
purring. Now that you have your love's attention, touch noses.
Playfully paw your love while moving in for a kiss. *Suggestions:
Wear a cat suit; paint whiskers on your face; curl up in your love's
lap, and arch your back if your love refuses to kiss you.*

♥ 43 ♥

EYELID KISS

While kissing your love, watch for his or her eyes to
close. Sweetly place a light kiss on each eyelid. *Helpful Hint: If
your love's eyes open, murmur that you have a surprise if he or she
closes them. They'll be shut before the blink of an eye.*

♥ 44 ♥

I'VE GOT A SECRET KISS

Whisper to your love how special he or she is to you, and then
seal your message with an ear kiss.

♥ 45 ♥

VALENTINE KISS

Celebrate Valentine's Day with kisses in the "V"
pattern of Morse code (short, short, short, long). *Idea: For fun,
synchronize your kisses with your humming of Beethoven's 5th
Symphony Overture.*

♥ 46 ♥

FOOTBALL KISS

After a pass during a football game, make a pass on your love.

♥ 47 ♥

SLEEPING BEAUTY KISS

Awaken your love from slumber with a tender kiss on the lips.

• 48 •

NO-CAL KISS

After dinner, give your love a no-calorie dessert…your lips.

• 49 •

CAB KISS

Hire a cab. Instruct the cab driver to drive around for
15 minutes while you and your love neck in the back seat.

• 50 •

HEAVY BREATHING KISS

Breathe heavily into your love's ear, then slide over to his or
her mouth and plant a steamer.

• 51 •

THE NECKLACE KISS

Deposit sweet kisses that circle your love's neck. *Hint 1:
Concentrate your kisses along the back of the neck. Hint 2: If the first
necklace went well, try a second.*

• 52 •

NOSEY NOSE KISS
Next time the two of you are outside on a cold day,
wrap your arms around your love's neck. Rub noses, then
sweetly kiss the tip of your love's nose.

• 53 •

NAPE OF NECK KISS
Surprise your love from behind. Move his or her hair
and/or pull down his or her collar to expose the back of your
love's neck. Kiss and blow on the nape of the neck.

• 54 •

EAR YE, EAR YE KISS
Kiss your love's ears. And while you're there, whisper something exciting.

• 55 •

NIGHT-AT-THE-MOVIES KISS

It's Friday night. Take your love to a movie. French
kiss his or her fingers to remove popcorn butter; nip kiss your
love's fingers during scary scenes; and hickey kiss his or
her fingers during love scenes.

• 56 •

BLANKET KISS

Wrap yourselves in a blanket outdoors on a blustery, winter
day and warm each other's lips.

• 57 •

LEMON KISS

Sprinkle two lemon wedges with sugar. Each take one.
On the count of three, bite into the wedge. Immediately kiss
each other's perfectly puckered lips.

♥ 58 ♥

SCHNAPPS KISS

Prepare two shots of Peppermint Schnapps. Have your
love take the first shot, and kiss him or her immediately after.
Next, you take the second shot and have your love
kiss you.

♥ 59 ♥

UNDER-THE-STARS KISSES

On the next beautiful clear night, find a place outside
for you and your love to sit and stare at the stars. Talk about
romantic times and kiss each other frequently.

♥ 60 ♥

OFF-THE-WALL, GOODBYE MORNING KISS

Think of a kiss you and your love have never shared. Then
send your love off in the morning with it. Say nothing if your
love asks the reason for the sexy send off. *Disclaimer:
It's guaranteed to make your love think about you all day. Not
responsible for what happens later.*

• 61 •

EAR WE GO AGAIN KISS

Lightly envelop your love's entire ear inside your mouth.
Let it fall out of your mouth slowly, earlobe last. Finish with a
light nibble on the earlobe.

• 62 •

GERMAN MORNING KISS

Write on the bathroom mirror in lipstick or soap
the following: "Morgenkuss" (German for "A morning kiss").
When your baffled love asks what it means, define it
right on the kisser.

• 63 •

CLANDESTINE KISS

Quietly tell your love you want to meet at a special
place (e.g. garden, back stairs, closet) at a specified time
without explaining why. When he or she arrives,
give your love a wonderfully romantic kiss. *Hint: Wear
something fun like a trench coat or towel.*

♥ 64 ♥

REARVIEW MIRROR KISS
Apply lipstick or chapstick to your lips. Kiss the
rearview mirror of your love's car, leaving a lip print for future
discovery.

♥ 65 ♥

BATHROOM TISSUE KISS
Plant a kiss on the first square of the bathroom
tissue roll and include a love note. Have it ready and waiting
for your love the next time he or she makes a trip to the
bathroom.

♥ 66 ♥

STARRY-EYED KISS
Kiss your love by starlight. *Here's how: On a beautiful
clear night, take your love outside. Bring a blanket, and tell your love
to keep his or her eyes open while you kiss. If you're lucky, you
might also see a shooting star.*

♥ 67 ♥

MUZZLE KISS

Put tape bandage over your mouth. Mumble and
motion for your love to remove it. When he or she asks what's
going on, tell your love you've been saving your lips all
day just for him or her. *Note: Don't attempt this kiss if you're a
known talker. Your love may welcome the silence.*

♥ 68 ♥

STRAWBERRY KISS

Hold a fresh, juicy strawberry between your lips. Beckon your
love to kiss it away.

♥ 69 ♥

SURPRISE PHONE CALL KISS

Surprise your love with an unexpected phone call
during the day. Don't say a word, but let loose with a long,
sloppy, kissing sound.

• 70 •

DRACULA KISS

Swoop down on your love unexpectedly. In a corny
Transylvanian accent, assert "I want to bite your neck," and
lightly bite his or her neck. *Idea: If your love agrees, give him
or her a hickey for show-and-tell at work the next day.*

• 71 •

CANDY KISS

Hide a piece of your love's favorite candy in your mouth,
and pass it to him or her during a kiss. *Note: Candy shouldn't be
runny or you will make a mess.*

• 72 •

WHIPPED CREAM KISS

Buy a can of whipped cream (yes, you know where this
is going). Fill each other's mouth. Kiss while trying to swallow
the whipped cream.

• 73 •

M'M M'M GOOD KISS

Entice your love into a romantic kiss. While kissing,
make the sound: M'm M'm M'm. Undoubtedly, such encour-
agement will make the kiss last longer.

• 74 •

PILLOW TALK KISS

Lie face-to-face with your love sharing a pillow. Whisper
mushy sentiments and kiss one another.

• 75 •

SECRET SUSPENSE KISS

Tell your love one morning you have a secret to
share later. Call your love during the day to remind him or
her to ask you about it. When your love gets home and
reminds you, whisper in your love's ear how much you love
him or her, and then kiss.

♥ 76 ♥

FROG KISS

In honor of St. Patrick's Day, dress in green, hop
around the house and occasionally ribbet. Eventually, your
love will ask why you are acting like a frog. Respond
that you're under a spell, and only a kiss from your true love
will turn you back into a handsome prince or princess.

♥ 77 ♥

NOODLE KISS

Go out for a romantic Italian dinner. Make sure one
of you orders something with long noodles. When the time is
right, each take an end of a noodle and draw it into your
mouths until your lips meet for a kiss.

♥ 78 ♥

CANDLE BLOW-OUT KISS

Eat dinner by candlelight. For dessert, blow out the
candle and make sparks. *Suggestion: If children are present, take a
candle and have your love follow you to a dark room. Close the
door and then blow out the candle.*

♥ 79 ♥

CANDID KISS

Somehow, somewhere, someway when he or she least expects
it...kiss your love.

♥ 80 ♥

FLINTSTONE KISS

Playfully decide to call each other Fred and Wilma today.
After you kiss your love holler, "Yaba daba do."

♥ 81 ♥

REVEILLE KISS

This kiss is a sexy wake-up call. Barely touch your lips
to your love's cheek and quietly hum reveille. The vibration
of your lips will tickle even the most sound
sleeper awake.

♥ 82 ♥

THE THREE C's KISS

Kiss your love on his or her chin, cheeks and collarbone.

♥ 83 ♥

OPEN ARMS KISS

Stand with your arms outstretched and invite your love to
come over for a kiss.

♥ 84 ♥

SLOW DANCE KISS

Pick a favorite slow dance song, and the two of you slow
dance; sway to the music of a favorite slow song, all the while
kissing one another.

♥ 85 ♥

COACH KISS

Don a cap, whistle and clipboard. Blow the whistle to
get your love's attention and indicate what kind of kiss you
want. Blow the whistle a second time and say, "All
right. Let's go!"

♥ 86 ♥

FRAGRANCE TESTING KISS

Dab some new fragrance on your neck and ask your love for
his or her opinion. As your love comes close for a whiff,
surprise him or her with a kiss.

♥ 87 ♥

ANNIVERSARY KISS

This year, on your wedding anniversary, re-enact your
wedding vows. Choose a romantic place where the two of you
can repeat them to one another. Conclude as you did the
first time…with a kiss.

♥ 88 ♥

KISSING UP KISS

Starting as low on your love as appropriate, kiss a
path upward. When you reach his or her lips, conclude with a
romantic lip kiss.

♥ 89 ♥

THE THREE N's KISS
Kiss your love on the navel, then the neck, and conclude with
a cute nose kiss.

♥ 90 ♥

LICORICE KISS
Buy a licorice whip. Each start eating from one
end until meeting at the middle where the two of you kiss.

♥ 91 ♥

FRONT DOOR KISS
Sneak outside and ring your doorbell. When your love
answers, surprise him or her with a single red rose and a kiss.

♥ 92 ♥

WAX LIPS KISS
Buy two pairs of big wax lips. You and your love
develop a unique wax lip technique. *Suggestion: Bite a hole out
of the middle.*

• 93 •

HOROSCOPE KISS

Have your love read his or her horoscope from a
newspaper or magazine. Of course you've been there first. The
original has been pasted over with your prediction of how
to kiss you today. *For example: Mars and Venus are
aligned, putting your kissing power at an all-time high. A vigorous
kissing session today is a must. If not acted on, your lips
could deflate and turn purple.*

• 94 •

RECORD-BREAKING KISS

Try for a personal kissing record with your love. Set a
timer for three minutes (more if you think possible) and kiss
until it goes off. *Suggestion: Make it more official by
finding a stop watch and a coach's cap.*

• 95 •

INSTANT REPLAY KISS

After a great kiss, tell your love you want an instant replay.

♥ 96 ♥

MOVIE KISS

Rent the movie with your favorite kissing scene (e.g.
Gone With The Wind, *Top Gun*). Fast forward to the scene so
you can show your love. After viewing, the two of you
try for perfect re-enactment. Replay the scene to see if the
two of you did it right. If not, keep trying.

♥ 97 ♥

EARLOBE KISS

Sneak up on your love from behind and put your arms around
his or her waist. Nibble on his or her earlobe.

♥ 98 ♥

HAMMOCK KISS

The two of you lie in an oversized hammock (positioning
yourselves without flipping over is half the fun). This is one of
the best inventions made to encourage kissing.

♥ 99 ♥

CHEEK-TO-CHEEK KISS

With your right cheek touching your love's left cheek,
roll toward each other's lips and kiss. *Note: We're talking about
the cheeks on our faces.*

♥ 100 ♥

FLOWER KISS

Have a single flower for your love when he or she
gets home. Present it while telling your love how very special
he or she is. Finish with a loving kiss.

♥ 101 ♥

THEME SONG KISS

We all have one special song that rekindles romantic feelings.
Find that song; play it for your love, and together create a
memorable kissing moment.

• 102 •

BACK RUB KISS
While kissing your love, rub his or her back. This is guaranteed to prolong the kiss.

• 103 •

FINGER WALKING KISS
Let your fingers do the walking to your love's lips for a kiss. If this kiss goes well, let your fingers do more walking.

• 104 •

FIRST KISS KISS
Without fighting, agree on how the first kiss between the two of you went. Set the stage as closely as possible to the original, and relive the memory. *Suggestion: If you still have the same clothes, wear them...if they still fit! Also, if you can remember any of the dialogue, try to recite it.*

♥ 105 ♥

THE THREE E's KISS

Choose any order, but kiss each of your love's ears, eyes and elbows.

♥ 106 ♥

SCARF KISS

Lasso your love with your scarf and round him or her up for a kiss

♥ 107 ♥

CARD KISS

Mail a romantic card to your love and seal it with a kiss.

♥ 108 ♥

HAIR COMBING KISS

Run your fingers through any and all hair on your love's head during a kiss.

• 109 •

BUBBLE BATH KISS
Have a bubble bath prepared for your love when he or
she gets home. Have a bowl of candy kisses within arm's reach
with a note saying, "For the real thing, just holler."

• 110 •

FULL MOON KISS
A full moon is very romantic. Take your love someplace
where the two of your can smooch by moonlight.

• 111 •

DRIVE-IN MOVIE KISS
Take your love to a drive-in movie. Kiss 'til the windows fog.

• 112 •

PERSONAL AD KISS
Take out a personal ad saying something like, "For the kiss
of a lifetime, (your love's name) call (your name). Circle the
ad and lay it on the table during dinner.

• 113 •

FORTUNE COOKIE KISS

Order take-out Chinese for dinner and exchange your love's fortune cookie with a fortune of your own design. *For instance: "For eternal luck and fame, tongue-dance with the person sitting across the table." Hint: Lightly tape the new fortune to the fortune currently in the cookie. As you pull out the old fortune, the new one will take its place.*

• 114 •

LICENSE PLATE KISS

The next time you and your love are in a car together, each pick and find an out-of-state license plate. See your plate, get a peck.

• 115 •

BUSBOY KISS

Dine with your love in a private corner of a restaurant. Agree that every time the busboy fills your water glass the two of you must kiss.

• 116 •

SWEAT KISS

You and your love go work out together. When both
of you are at your sweatiest, put your pumped-up arms around
each other and share a wet, slippery kiss.

• 117 •

ICE CREAM KISS

Share an ice cream cone with simultaneous licking.
If tongue movements and closeness don't get the two of you
kissing, think of how cold and wonderful your love's
mouth tastes and go in for a smooch.

• 118 •

KISS-THE-COOK KISS

Spell out the words "Kiss the Cook" with food and
serve to your love. *Note: You can use raisins on oatmeal, croutons
on salad, olives on a pizza or whatever you can dream up.*

♥ 119 ♥

COFFEE KISS

Serve coffee to your love, then ask, "Will it be one kiss
or two?"

♥ 120 ♥

GIFT KISS

Arrange to have flowers, balloons, cookies or whatever
sent to your love at work. The attached note should simply
state "S. W. A. K." (Sealed With A Kiss).

♥ 121 ♥

COUPON KISS

Make kissing coupons and slip them into your love's
purse or briefcase. *Ideas: make coupons good for certain locations in
the house. Spray them with your signature cologne or perfume.
Describe the kind of kiss each coupon entitles your love
to receive.*

• 122 •

BANNER KISS

Make a huge banner saying "Kiss Me" with an equally
huge arrow pointing downward. Hang it from the ceiling and
stand under the arrow when your love arrives.

• 123 •

PHOTO KISS

Stage a photo session and capture a photo of the two of
you kissing for posterity. Find a camera with a timer, or go to a
photo booth. *Suggestion: Dress in different costumes for different
looks (Bikers, Bonnie & Clyde, Coneheads).*

• 124 •

CUDDLE & COO KISS

Prepare a cozy place on the floor for the two of you to
cuddle and watch TV. Have lots of pillows, a blanket, a handy
place to set the wine bottle and glasses, and dim the lights.
Agree to kiss during every commercial.

♥ 125 ♥

ON-THE-PHONE KISS

Kiss your love while he or she talks on the phone.
Keep kissing him or her while your love wriggles and tries to
keep composure. *Warning: Make sure the phone call isn't
important.*

♥ 126 ♥

GRAPE KISS

Feed each other grapes. Put one between your lips and signal
your love to come and get it.

♥ 127 ♥

MORTICIA KISS

This one's named after the *Addams Family* television
show. Begin kissing your love's hand. Work up to the crook of
his or her arm, lingering for a moment. Continue up the
arm to the shoulder. Work over to the neck and up to the ear
for a final ear kiss.

♥ 128 ♥

BEVERAGE KISS

Surprise your love by serving his or her favorite drink.
Just before handing it to your love, deliver a sweet kiss and
say, "I wanted to touch your lips before this did."

♥ 129 ♥

TRYST KISS

Get the business card of a restaurant or hotel where
you have made rendezvous plans. Kiss or draw an "X" on it.
Attach a note saying, "There's more where this came
from," and include the time and address of the intended tryst.
Spray the note with your favorite cologne or perfume, and
hide it in your love's purse or briefcase.

♥ 130 ♥

KISS À L'ORANGE

In conjunction with your fresh-squeezed morning
orange juice, have two orange quarters cut. Each of you place
an orange quarter in your mouth, peel side showing,
and kiss.

• 131 •

MEMORIES KISS

With the song *Memories* playing in the background,
tell your love you want the two of you to create some kissing
memories.

• 132 •

CHEER KISS

In the spirit of football season, lead your love through
the following cheer: "Ready. O.K. Give me a "K." Give me an
"I." Give me an "S." Give me another "S." What does
that spell? Well, ready? O.K. Give me a kiss." *Suggestion: Dress
as a cheerleader or yell leader complete with pompons or a
megaphone. You can even try to make your body look like the letters
as you yell them.*

• 133 •

DINNER MINT KISS

After dinner, position a dinner mint between your lips.
Sweet-talk your love to come kiss it away.

• 134 •

RED "X" KISS

Make a large red "X" and put it on the floor. Inform
your love that "X" marks the spot. When you stand on it, you
wish to be kissed. *Suggestion: Keep this "X" around.*
You two can make a game out of standing on it when either one wants
a kiss.

• 135 •

REFRIGERATOR KISS

For dinner, the two of you sit in front of your open
refrigerator (stocked with each other's favorite foods) and feed
each other. No napkins allowed. Kissing is the only way
to clean each other's face and hands. *Note: Cover the floor with*
a sheet or towel for easy clean-up afterward.

• 136 •

KISSING SHOWER

Invite your love to a kissing shower. A kissing shower is
showering your love with kisses in the shower.

♥ 137 ♥

WALKMAN KISS

Kiss each other while wearing *Walkmans*. *Note: It's better if you're both tuned to the same type of music.*

♥ 138 ♥

DANCING FRENCH KISS

Find some romantic music and have your tongues dance to the beat.

♥ 139 ♥

HAIR-HOLD KISS

Kiss your love and run your fingers up the back of his or her neck until your fingers fill with hair. Lightly grab the hair and hold onto it throughout the kiss. *Note: If your love's hair is up, unfasten it so it falls down. Warning: don't do this kiss in the morning if your love has just fixed his or her hair for the day.*

• 140 •

KISSING PARTY
Invite your love to a kissing party. Make out an invitation, to include the time and place. Also state that the door prize is a French kiss, and that hors d'oeuvres will be chocolate kisses.

• 141 •

MOUTH WHISPERING KISS
Chico Marx has a famous quote: "I wasn't kissing her, I was whispering in her mouth." Whisper a sweet message to your love while kissing.

• 142 •

LIFE SAVER KISS
A *Life Saver* candy is a great kissing prop. It has a hole to touch tongues through, tastes wonderful, and eventually dissolves. Pop a *Life Saver* in your mouth, and have fun kissing your love until it vanishes.

♥ 143 ♥

PREOCCUPIED HANDS KISS

Place something cumbersome in your love's
hands (e.g. salad bowls, vases, cartons of eggs). With his or
her hands incapacitated, move in for the kiss of your
choosing.

♥ 144 ♥

TUSH KISS

Kiss your love while grabbing his or her tush.

♥ 145 ♥

OFF-SEASON KISSLETOE

Mistletoe works all year long. Find some mistletoe
(fake works too) and hang it over the shower, kitchen sink, or
have some in your pocket ready to whip out when the
moment is right.

• 146 •

FOREWARNED KISS
Leave your love a note alerting him or her about
where you will be kissing him or her later. When you two
meet next…watch out!

• 147 •

HIS & HER CAR KISS
Secretly park your two cars bumper to bumper as if kissing.
Tell your love the cars are at it again and to come see.

• 148 •

TOWEL KISS
When your love finishes showering, be waiting with a
warm towel to dry him or her off. Kiss the spots you missed
with the towel.

• 149 •

S.W.A.K. KISS
Write a love letter and seal it with a kiss.

• 150 •

ROSE & VIOLET KISS

Place a rose and a violet on your love's pillow with the
note: "Roses are red. Violets are blue. I may be at work, but
my thoughts are of kissing you."

• 151 •

COMIC STRIP KISS

Look for a comic strip that ends with a kissing scene
(e.g. Apt. 3-D, Blondie). Paste your own dialogue onto the
strip and leave it in an obvious place for your love to
find and read.

• 152 •

PECK-A-BOO KISS

Sneak up on your love and cover his or her eyes with
your hands. When you uncover them, plant a peck on his or
her lips.

♥ 153 ♥

PARKING KISS

With your love in the car, find a romantic place to park and neck.

♥ 154 ♥

KISS CERTIFICATE

Design a certificate that says, "This certificate entitles the holder to one long, romantic kiss with his or her favorite kissing partner." *Warning: Make sure it is redeemable with you only.*

♥ 155 ♥

UNSCHEDULED KISS

Break your weekly routine by going out for dinner or to a movie. Ask for a quiet corner or sit in the back of the theater and frequently give each other little love pecks.

• 156 •

CAFE DE KISS
Invite your love to your private restaurant with only
one table for two. Feature a menu of your love's favorite food.
At the end of the meal, present a bill—payable in kisses.

• 157 •

ANSWERING MACHINE KISS
After the beep, leave a long, sloppy kissing sound and the
message, "There's more where that came from!"

• 158 •

NAIL KISSES
Softly kiss each fingernail on your love's hands. If your love
enjoyed it, continue down to the toenails.

• 159 •

TOAST KISS
Decorate your love's toast one morning with jam in the shape
of lips or "XXX" written in cinnamon or butter.

• 160 •

WEEK OF KISSES
Write five love notes about how much you love
kisses. Mark them "Personal and Confidential," and then seal
each with a kiss or "XXX." Mail one a day (beginning
Saturday) to your love at home or at the office.

• 161 •

SANDWICH KISSES
Decorate your love's sandwich today with kisses.
Make "Xs" out of tomatoes, red bell peppers, beets or whatever. Take it one step further and decorate the plate with "Xs"
made from carrot sticks, cheese twists or any other
imaginative edible item you can find.

• 162 •

KISSLETOE
Any chance you get during Christmas, pull out the mistletoe
and treat your love to a kiss.

• 163 •

SIGNAL A KISS

The two of you agree to a private "I want a kiss"
signal to be used at parties or in public. Practice using it
several times so you'll remember it for frequent use in
the future. *Signal suggestions: A long blink, lip tracing with your
finger, tugging at your hair.*

• 164 •

TACKLE KISS

Tackle and wrestle your love onto the couch or bed. When
your love is pinned down, plant him or her a big ol' kiss.

• 165 •

EVENTFUL KISS

Tell your love that for a kiss, you will provide a big
surprise. Upon receipt, present your love with a pair of tickets
to his or her favorite event (e.g. football, opera, theater).
Whether you like it or not, agree to go with your love.

• 166 •

MORNING MIRROR KISS

Let the bathroom mirror display your desire for kisses. With a
bar of soap, draw "Xs" around the edges of the mirror.

• 167 •

BUTTON KISS

Find a place that will take your picture and put it on a
button. Have them zoom in for a close-up of your puckered
lips. Pin the button to your love's coat.

• 168 •

DEDICATION KISS

Call the radio station your love listens to and ask for
an announcement that you're in need of a kiss from your love.
(Obviously, tell them your love's name.) *Suggestion: Just in
case your love misses the message, tape it for posterity.*

• 169 •

MAP KISS
Draw a map to a private place and mark the spot
with a red "X." Roll up the map, tie it with a bow and attach
the following note: "A kiss awaits you where 'X' marks
the spot. Please have your lips warmed up and ready to go at
(time)."

• 170 •

TELEGRAM KISS
Send a telegram to your love with a loving message requesting
his or her tender lips as soon as possible.

• 171 •

BOOKMARK KISS
Make a bookmark with kisses all over it. Place it in the book
your love is currently reading.

♥ 172 ♥

WRITER'S KISS

Use your imagination to write a kissing scene. Make it as lusty as you feel comfortable with, and include dialogue. Mail it or FAX it (if secure) to your love with a note: "Rehearsal begins at (time) sharp."

♥ 173 ♥

PHOTO TOUCH-UP KISS

Find a profile photo of each of you. Cut along the profile line, and glue the two photos together so you look like you're kissing. On the bottom, write: "Wish we were kissing right now."

♥ 174 ♥

SNACK OF KISSES

Prepare a snack that sends a clear message you want to be kissed. Include chocolate kisses, wax lips, strawberries, X-shaped pretzels, lip shapes cut from red bell peppers, etc. The more bizarre the selection, the better.

• 175 •

LIP PRINT KISS

Have a photograph made of your lips. Put the lip print in a
small stand-up frame. Give it to your love to take to
the office.

• 176 •

FILE-A-KISS

Create kissing files in your love's personal home
computer (you may need a computer-friendly friend to help).
In his or her most frequently used directory, name files
with tantalizing titles such as, "Smooch," "Hot Lips,"
"Frenchy," etc. Inside each file write special love messages
signed with "Xs" for kisses. *Idea: Add one new file to this directory
every month.*

• 177 •

CORNERSTONE KISS

Next time you walk around the corner of a building surprise
your love with a spontaneous kiss.

• 178 •

CAR WINDOW KISSES

Take a bar of soap and write "Kiss," "Smack," or
"Smooch," all over the windows of your love's car. Be sure to
write the words backwards so they can be read
from inside the car. *Tip: A hose or good rain will wash the
windows clean.*

• 179 •

MANNEQUIN KISS

The next time you see your love, strike a pose and don't
blink. *Have a sign around your neck that reads: "Breathe life into me
by performing mouth-to-mouth resuscitation."*

• 180 •

DESSERT KISS

Find a place that serves your love's favorite dessert.
During dessert, feed each other and agree to kiss between
bites.

♥ 181 ♥

CUPID'S BOW KISS
Kiss your love tenderly on his or her Cupid's Bow (romantic
name given to the outline of the upper lip).

♥ 182 ♥

UNDERWEAR KISS
Men: find her lingerie drawer and draw "XXX", with
her lip-liner pencil, on her undergarments. Women: locate his
undershorts and leave a lip print, in lipstick, on each pair.

♥ 183 ♥

UPSIDE DOWN KISS
This kiss will gaurantee laughter. Belly-side down,
both of you bend over the side of the bed next to each other
until your heads are resting upside down on the floor.
With your blood rushing to your head, wait until you are each
beet red, and then kiss.

• 184 •

ALARM KISS

Set a timer or the alarm clock to go off at an odd
hour. When the alarm sounds, inform your love that "It's
time." When he or she asks for what, respond, "Time
for a kiss."

• 185 •

BATHROOM SURPRISE KISS

Float a morning kiss in the commode. Here's how. On
a white sheet of tissue, blot your lips or draw "Xs" with a red
waterproof, felt-tip pen. Peel the two plies apart, and
discard the bottom one. Carefully place the tissue on the
water's surface and close the lid.

• 186 •

BELLY KISS

With your hands behind your heads, stick out your bare
bellies and navel kiss.

• 187 •

STRANGER KISS

If you're preppie, dress sexy. If you're blonde, be a
brunette. You become a stranger who must have a kiss from
your love. *Idea: Don't just look different, act differently. If you're
loud, speak softly. If you're shy, be aggressive.*

• 188 •

GIANT CANDY KISS

Buy a large candy kiss. Make a personal streamer come
out of the top. Have it delivered to your love at home or at
the office.

• 189 •

GROCERY SHOPPING KISS

Go grocery shopping together. Make a game out of
stealing kisses when no one is looking (e.g. behind the freezer
door, leaning over the produce, waiting in the check-
out line).

• 190 •

WELCOME HOME KISS
Greet your love at the door with a big warm kiss and
cheerful "Glad you're home." Take his or her baggage, direct
to a comfortable chair, remove shoes, and hand him or
her the remote control or the paper.

• 191 •

THE UNKNOWN KISSER
Appear wearing a brown paper bag over your
head with holes cut out for your eyes and mouth. Put your lips
through the mouth hole, lip-smack your love, and then
dance away. Come back into the room without the bag, and
play dumb about what just happened.

• 192 •

LAPEL KISS
Glide your hands under the lapels of your love's
coat or jacket. Then, lightly grasping the lapels, draw your
love toward you for a kiss.

⬩ 193 ⬩

CAR DOOR KISS
Just before you or your love opens the car door, give an unexpected kiss.

⬩ 194 ⬩

LAUNDRY KISS
Heap all the laundry into one big pile. Grab your love, wrestle him or her to the pile on the floor, and then roll and kiss together in the pile. *Note: Clean laundry preferable.*

⬩ 195 ⬩

BASTILLE DAY KISS
In honor of Bastille Day....You guessed it—a French kiss!

⬩ 196 ⬩

PULSE KISS
Gently take your love's hand and turn it over to expose the inner wrist. Read your love's pulse with your lips.

▾ 197 ▾

EXALTED KISS

Next time your unsuspecting love sits in a chair,
kneel in front of him or her. With your arms and torso
moving up and down, chant, "I worship the ground you walk
on." Conclude with a light kiss atop his or her feet.

▾ 198 ▾

MID-CONVERSATION KISS

In the middle of the next casual conversation with
your love, unexpectedly close your eyes and pucker your lips.
If your love asks what's going on, pucker your lips even
more. If your love still doesn't catch on, ask for a kiss and wait
for receipt.

▾ 199 ▾

NO-NAPKIN KISSES

Cook or order a dinner that's messy to eat. The rule for
the evening is "No Napkins." Any dirty faces or fingers must
be kissed clean.

• 200 •

CITATION KISS

Dress up like a cop and slap your love with a citation for negligent kissing. The fine is your favorite kiss to be paid in 30 seconds, or the fine doubles. *Ideas: Make a badge that reads "Kissing Patrol." Read your love his or her kissing rights and explain that the offense requires an official frisking.*

• 201 •

STICK-UP KISSES

In your love's kitchen, office or personal room, hide as many stick-up notes with lip prints or "XXXs" as you can. Put them in drawers, on lights, inside the pots and pans, under pillows, etc. Every "stick-up" is redeemable for the real thing.

• 202 •

TIED-UP KISS

Using a scarf or necktie, loosely tie your love's hands behind his or her back. Now in control, take the lead and kiss your love. *Caution: this is supposed to be fun, not frightening.*

• 203 •

KISSES IN THE CLOUDS
Buy dry ice. Create a cloud effect in one of your
rooms. Inform love you have always wanted to be kissed in
the clouds.

• 204 •

TARZAN & JANE KISS
Make it jungle night at your place. Put all the plants
in one room. Serve fruits, nuts and berries, and wear jungle
attire. Hang rope for vines. Speak monosyllabically, and
tell your Tarzan or Jane, "Me want kiss now."

• 205 •

CROWN KISS
Make a royal crown for your love. In a ceremony
that you design, designate your love as your king or queen.
Place the crown on your love's head; kiss him or her and
then say, "Now I've officially kissed royalty."

• 206 •

VOCAL KISS
When the two of you kiss, use all the sounds you can think of
while kissing (e.g. slurping, smacking, sucking, hissing,
humming, grunting, moaning, sighing).

• 207 •

STOLEN KISS
Traditionally, young boys steal kisses from coy young
girls. Well, young or old, male or female, steal a kiss from your
love today.

• 208 •

PATH-OF-KISSES
Cut out lip shapes and place them on the floor
leading to one of your love's favorite destinations. When your
love asks what the path is for, explain, "I decided to kiss
the ground you walk on."

• 209 •

KISS & TELL KISS

After kissing your love today, say he or she is a great kisser
and tell why.

• 210 •

SUGAR KISS

Lightly moisten your lips and pat them with powdered sugar.
Now, find your love and give a sweet kiss.

• 211 •

BRACELET KISS

Sweetly take your love's hand. Place tender kisses all the way
around the wrist.

• 212 •

SIGH KISS

After kissing your love, close your eyes, and give a big
sigh as if to say, "That kiss was just fabulous." Then ask your
love if he or she will kiss you like that again.

• 213 •

KISSING SCHOOL

Proclaim yourself the professor of kissing. Lecture to
your love on the fine points of kissing. Give a kissing assign-
ment, and tell your love he or she will be graded. Of
course, give him or her an A+.

• 214 •

LUSTY KISS

Decide that you have an intense desire and need for
a kiss from your love. Then, go find him or her and satisfy
your lust.

• 215 •

NETWORK KISS

Is your love a subscriber to one of the personal
computer networks? If so, send him or her kisses through the
electronic mail function. If not, just post a note for all to
read espousing your love's puckering prowess.

♥ 216 ♥

FISH KISS

If you're out fishing, ordering fish, or near a fish, the
moment calls for a fish kiss. Both separate your teeth and suck
in your cheeks until the corners of your mouth meet.
The two of your are now ready to kiss with fish lips.

♥ 217 ♥

GYM KISS

Next time the two of you work out in a gym, keep
an eye out for a strategic time to surprise your love with a kiss
(e.g. during floor exercises, while stretching, or when using
weight machines).

♥ 218 ♥

ELEVATOR KISS

Next time the two of you are alone in an elevator,
embrace and kiss until seconds before the elevator doors open.

♥ 219 ♥

30-YARD DASH KISS

You've seen this kiss in movies and soap operas, so why
not your life too? Stand about 30 yards apart. Now run toward
each other with your arms stretched wide. When you
meet, wrap your arms around each other and kiss. *Suggestion:
One can pick up the other and twirl in a circle during the kiss.*

♥ 220 ♥

CRY-BABY KISS

The movie *Cry Baby* had great dialogue leading up to
a kiss. Make flash cards of the following dialogue, and the two
of you re-enact the scene.

(Standing, arms around each other.)
Cry-Baby: Kiss me, kiss me hard.
Ingenue: I've never French kissed before.
*Cry-Baby: You just open your mouth and I open mine and we wiggle
our tongues together.*
Ingenue: I won't get mononucleosis will I?
(The two of you kiss)

• 221 •

TRENCH COAT KISS

The two of you agree to wear trench coats and rendezvous at a pre-determined place for a "flashing." What each
of you wear or don't wear under the trench coat is
the surprise. On the count of three, flash each other, then
embrace and kiss.

• 222 •

EAREKA! KISS

An alternative to blowing into you love's ear. Put your
lips near his or her ear and lightly inhale through your mouth
the same way you suck on a straw. Top off this fabulous
sensation with a kiss.

• 223 •

BODY PARTS KISS

Blindfold and place your love's hands behind his or her
back. Have your love kiss a part of your body, and guess which
part it is. After three correct guesses, it's your turn.

• 224 •

ETCH-A-KISS

If the two of you love back rubs, this kiss is perfect.
Etch on your love's back where you'd like to be kissed. After
he or she kisses you, it's your love's turn to etch on your
back where he or she wants to be kissed.

• 225 •

VARIETY PACK KISSES

Buy one of those cereal variety packs, put your own
labels on each box, and have it waiting at your love's breakfast table. Name ideas could be Sugar Frosted Lips, Corn
Smacks, Rice Hickeys.

• 226 •

RESUSCITATION KISS

Tell your love you're feeling faint, and need immediate
mouth-to-mouth resuscitation. Make your love kiss you a very
long time before showing life.

• 227 •

MUSIC KISSES

Pick one of the following songs. Find your love,
play the tune, and kiss until it ends. *Soul Provider* by Michael
Bolton, *Unforgettable* by Natalie Cole, or *Don't Make Me
Wait for Love* by Kenny G.

• 228 •

SNIFF & KISS

Dab cologne or perfume on spots you would like your
love to kiss. Tell your love to sniff out your favorite spots to
be kissed, saying how many spots are optional.

• 229 •

TIP-OF-THE-NOSE KISS

Put your love's favorite substance on the tip of your
nose (e.g. chocolate frosting, whipped cream, peanut butter,
cheese spread). Tell your love if he or she wants it, it
will have to be kissed off.

• 230 •

MAIL KISS

Collect the mail. Sort out your love's mail and tie it with a bow. When your love asks for it, hold it behind your back until you get a kiss.

• 231 •

SCOTCH WEDDING KISS

This kiss dates back to the 19th Century. Grab your love by the ears and kiss him or her on the lips.

• 232 •

CHIN-UP KISS

Somehow get your love to look up at the sky or the ceiling. With your love's chin raised, either kiss her neck in the curve beneath her chin, or kiss his Adam's apple.

♥ 233 ♥

NECK-NECKING KISS

Neck with your love, but only kiss each other's necks. Take turns and kiss up the side of the neck, under the ear, along the hairline, etc.

♥ 234 ♥

MEDIEVAL INDIA'S 7 IDEAL KISSES

Try this seven-kiss sequence on your love, then decide if it's ideal. Lower lip, both eyes, both cheeks, the head, then mouth, both breasts and then each shoulder.

♥ 235 ♥

MOUTHWASHING KISS

Hide both toothbrushes this morning. Instead, put toothpaste on each other's tongues and French clean the other's mouth.

• 236 •

POUTING KISS

Catch your love's attention by sporting big pouting lips.
When asked what's wrong, say you want a kiss. Have your
love kiss your pouting lips.

• 237 •

COUCH CORNERING KISS

In 1936, author Hugh Morris proclaimed the best way
to kiss your love was to first corner him or her against the arm
of a sofa. "First flatter them, then grab hold and finally
move in for the kiss."

• 238 •

BLOW FISH KISS

The two of you puff out your cheeks with air. Now,
zero in for a kiss with your love, keeping your eyes open and
trying not to laugh.

♥ 239 ♥

WIDE-EYED KISS

If you kiss with your eyes closed, tell your love to keep eyes
open and the two of you kiss wide-eyed.

♥ 240 ♥

BLACKOUT KISS

Throw the breaker or remove all the light bulbs. The
two of you have a romantic evening kissing and cuddling with
no electric light, firelight or candlelight.

♥ 241 ♥

VIDEO KISS

Make a video on the subject of kissing and give it
to your love. If you're shy, wear a disguise or a paper sack.
Reminisce about your favorite kisses together and/or
reveal a fantasy kiss you would like to receive. Have your
love view it alone.

▾ 242 ▾

TOAST KISS II

You know that pretzel position that the bride and groom
get into when they toast at their wedding? Well, why not do
it when there's no wedding? Each holding a glass, thread
your right arm through your love's right arm. You two should
now be face-to-face. Make a toast, sip, then kiss.

▾ 243 ▾

HIEROGLYPHIC COMPUTER KISSES

The next time your love leaves his or her computer unlocked, type kissing hieroglyphics on the screen. *Note: Use
your imagination to come up with kissing hieroglyphics of
your own. Some examples below include:*

:)	*Forehead Kiss*
:*)	*Cheek Kiss*
:o	*Little Kiss*
: ()	*Huge Kiss*
: P	*Tongue Kiss*
; o	*Winking Kiss*
;D	*Happy Kiss*
]:o	*Devilish Kiss*

• 244 •

VOW KISS

Think of a vow you would like to share with your
love and memorize it. Then, standing a few feet apart, face
your love hand-in-hand, and recite your vow. Afterward, both close eyes and lean forward until your lips meet
in a kiss.

• 245 •

LIP-CLIMBING KISS

For those of you who like climbing, this kiss is for you.
Begin by placing a kiss on your love's lower lip while he or she
places a kiss on your upper lip. Whoever's kissing the
lower lip gets to move to the upper lip.

• 246 •

LIP-O-SUCTION KISS

This kiss may not remove fat, but it's a lot more fun.
Lightly suck your love's upper lip, while he or she sucks your
lower lip.

• 247 •

CORNER KISS

Corner your love and kiss the corners of his or her mouth.

• 248 •

TULIPS (TWO-LIP) KISS

Kiss with your two warm, moist lips enclosing your love's lips. *Idea: Preface this kiss with a note attached to a tulip flower that reads: "Two-lips waiting for you."*

• 249 •

FACE BATH KISS

Bathe your love's face in kisses today.

• 250 •

COMBAT KISS

Next time the two of you deep kiss, have a spirited tongue battle to gain the territory of the other's mouth.

⋆ 251 ⋆

VACUUM KISS

Inform your love his or her face needs dusting
and you have just the tool to fix the problem. With your
love's curiosity piqued, turn your lips into a human
vacuum. While lightly sucking in, move your lips all over
your love's face.

⋆ 252 ⋆

PUSH-UP KISSES

For you exercise freaks, here's a kiss you can do while
working out. Have your love lie down face-up. You get in the
push-up position over your love. Each time you lower
yourself, kiss your love. Your love can help by keeping count.
Go for a record.

⋆ 253 ⋆

FRENCH HUMMER KISS

While the two of you French kiss, one or both of you make
humming sounds. The vibration is great.

• 254 •

TONGUE TIP TANGO KISS

Tell your love to close his or her eyes and stick out his
or her tongue. Gently tap the tip of your love's tongue with
your own.

• 255 •

SUCTION KISS

Surprise your love during a deep kiss by creating a
suction between your two mouths. Guaranteed to extend the
length of the kiss.

• 256 •

BABY BOTTLE KISS

Deep kiss your love, drawing his or her tongue into your
mouth and then lightly sucking on it.

❣ 257 ❣

THE HOOVER KISS

Kiss your love to form a tight seal. Both of you then
suck inward to create a vacuum inside your mouths. *Caution:
Reverse the suction before trying to separate. Do not hold this
kiss for too long; it can become painful.*

❣ 258 ❣

ROOF KISS

Find the highest roof possible and spend a romantic
evening on it. Bring a blanket, wine and anything else you
want. Spend the evening enjoying the view and each
other's lips.

❣ 259 ❣

CIRCLE KISS

This kiss is a fun variation during a long necking
session. Using the tip of your tongue trace your love's upper,
then lower lip in a circular motion. Alternate tracing the
inner lips with the outer lips.

• 260 •

PING PONG KISS

This is a fun game to play when kissing your love. Form
a tight seal between your two sets of lips. Puff out your cheeks,
and blow air into your love's mouth, causing his or her
cheeks to puff out. Your love, in turn, blows the air back to
you, causing your cheeks to again puff out. Do this back
and forth 'til your laughter breaks the seal.

• 261 •

TREE HOUSE KISS

If you have kids, you probably have a tree house. But
if not, find a friend who wouldn't mind letting you and your
love borrow it for a few hours. Get there first and
make it cozy with whatever you think is appropriate. Have
wine chilling in a bucket that you can pull up with
a rope. Once your love arrives, pull up the ladder, cuddle
and kiss.

• 262 •

BODY JOINT KISS

Make a game out of finding, then kissing the inside of
every body joint on your love (e.g. wrist, arm, neck). *Idea: Find
Gray's Anatomy for a complete listing.*

• 263 •

THERMOSTAT KISS

Without your love knowing, turn down the thermostat.
When your love complains of being cold, come to the rescue
with warm arms and lips.

• 264 •

ADD-A-KISS KISS

Begin with a kiss to your love. Have your love
repeat your kiss then add one of his or her own. You repeat
the sequence and add a new one at the end. The first
one to incorrectly repeat the kissing sequence has to kiss the
other's feet.

• 265 •

FRENCH EAR KISS

You know what a French kiss is. Well, just replace your love's
lips for an ear. *Caution: Monitor your moisture level.*

• 266 •

SHOOTER KISS

Cut out a pair of lips or buy some wax lips. Attach the
lips to the projectile of a dart gun. Hunt down your love and
shoot a kiss.

• 267 •

HIGH CARD KISS

With a deck of cards, each cut the deck. Whoever has
the highest card must kiss the loser. (Is there really a loser?)

• 268 •

90-DEGREE KISS

With right cheek on your love's left cheek and nose
tips touching, kiss each other out of the sides of your mouth.

♥ 269 ♥

CEREAL KISS

Make the "K" on that *Special K* box stand for "Kisses."
Replace the box's contents with special kissing paraphernalia
like candy *Kisses*, toast-shaped lips, or any other clever
things you can think of. Have the box waiting on your love's
breakfast table.

♥ 270 ♥

NECK CARESS KISS

With your right hand, slowly and gently move your
hand along your love's neck, passing the ear and concluding
with your hand cupping the back of the head.
Now use this hand to draw your love toward you for a
warm kiss.

♥ 271 ♥

EARRESISTIBLE KISS

Trace your love's ear with your nose, then conclude with an
ear kiss.

• 272 •

AIRPLANE KISS

Arms spread, lips puttering, execute a final-flight approach
for a four-point landing on your love's lips. *Idea: Wear a beanie
with a propeller, and cut out a cardboard wing-tail to wear.*

• 273 •

KISSING PLANT

Create a kissing plant. Tie kissing symbols to a living plant, or
make a special plant of your own. Give it to your love as
a reminder to kiss you. *Hint: Move the plant around from time to
time so your love will be inspired to remember.*

• 274 •

LAPP KISS

The Lapps of Northern Europe are famous for their
unique kisses. Try it on your love. Cover your love's mouth
and nose with your lips, and give a big, noisy kiss.
Of course, your love should be allowed to try it on you next.

• 275 •

STEAMING KISSES

Kiss the mirror in your bathroom with *Vaseline* lips.
When the mirror steams up, the lips stand out. This is a nice
surprise when your love gets out of the shower.

• 276 •

BATHING SURPRISE KISS

Fill the bathtub or shower stall with red balloons.
Upon removal of balloons your love will find a big set of
puckered lips on the floor.

• 277 •

KISSES IN RETURN

Give your love self-addressed stamped postcards.
Instruct your love to mail one each time he or she thinks of
kissing you, but can't be there.

• 278 •

SURPRISE BATH KISS

Surprise your love with a bubble bath. Have a rubber ducky
floating with a big lip print on its bill.

• 279 •

CHRYSANTHEMUM KISS

Chinese say that if you wipe your lips with a chrysanthemum
after drinking wine and then give the flower to your
love, he or she will be yours forever. Well…what are you
waiting for?

• 280 •

INDEX FINGER KISS

With the index finger of your right hand placed under your
love's chin, draw it in for a warm, soft, lip-to-lip kiss.

♥ 281 ♥

SPINE KISS

Next time the two of you are wrapped in a kissing
embrace, trace your love's spine from neck to waist with your
fingers.

♥ 282 ♥

JOGGING KISS

The next time the two of you jog together, try kissing
each other without slowing down. *Hints: Your pace needs to be
the same, both need to be on the same foot and the kiss can't
last long, otherwise your breathing could be affected.*

♥ 283 ♥

ICE CUBE KISSES

Cut out paper lips. Place one in each square of an ice
cube tray; fill with water, and freeze. Leave in the freezer for
your love to find, or float the cubes in your love's
favorite drink.

• 284 •

TEETH-COUNT KISS
Count how many teeth your love has, using your tongue.

• 285 •

NO-OCCASION KISS
Today send an unexpected red rose to your love.
Attach a lip print or "XXX" for no reason other than to say "I
love you."

• 286 •

PIG KISS
Burrow your nose and mouth into the nape of your love's neck
and snort like a pig.

• 287 •

THINKING-OF-YOU KISS

Take a handkerchief, mark with lip prints or "Xs", spray
with your personal perfume or cologne, and tuck it into your
love's suitcase the next time he or she leaves town.
Idea: Include a note that reads: "Think of me."

• 288 •

PRESSURE KISS

Give your love a lip-to-lip kiss, but apply significant
pressure. *Note: Don't apply so much pressure that you could damage
dental work.*

• 289 •

SWING KISS

Find a swing and seat your love in it. Every time your love
swings near you, try for a kiss.

♥ 290 ♥

KISS CODES

You and your love create a code that signals a kiss is immi-
nent (e.g. three hand squeezes, two winks, a short cough).

♥ 291 ♥

MOVIE RENTAL KISS

There is the Cannes Film Festival, so why not feature
your own home film festival? Pick a festival theme such as
Astaire & Rogers, 15th Century Romance and/or
Action. Turn on the VCR and serve popcorn or your favorite
snack. Neck in the privacy of your own home.

♥ 292 ♥

TAPE RECORDED KISS

Leave a tape recorder out with a sign telling your love
to push the "Play" button. Have recorded a big, sloppy, kissing
sound, a fantasy kiss, or a description of how you want your
love to kiss you the next time you're together.

• 293 •

CALENDAR KISS
Next time your love leaves town, place a calendar
in the luggage. Mark the days your love will be gone with red
"Xs" or kisses. The return day is marked with a
"Look Out."

• 294 •

PAVLOV'S DOG KISS
If you pucker your lips at your love, chances are you'll get
kissed. Try this theory.

• 295 •

FORTUNE TELLER KISS
Make your own kissing Tarot Cards, or go to a
fortune teller with a well-greased palm. Your love's future is
bleak unless a romantic kiss is bestowed on the love of
his or her life.

▾ 296 ▾

KISS OF INNOCENCE

Standing a few feet apart and facing your love, place his
or her hands in yours. Both close your eyes and lean forward
until lips meet in a kiss.

▾ 297 ▾

PINCH KISS

During a deep kiss with your love, run your tongue between
his or her cheek and gums.

▾ 298 ▾

GAS STATION KISS

Next time your love's car needs gas, offer to pump gas in
exchange for the kiss of your choice.

▾ 299 ▾

FIREWORKS KISS

Set off fireworks for your love. Like in the movies, kiss each
other while they explode.

♥ 300 ♥

CATWOMAN KISS

Catwoman gave Batman a kiss he'll never forget in the
movie *Batman Returns*. If you know the kiss, try it out on your
love. If you don't, rent the movie, then repeat the scene
after the two of you watch it together.

♥ 301 ♥

DIET KISS

Does your love want to lose weight? Offer to eliminate
hunger pains with kisses. This is proven to be a great distrac-
tion from food.

♥ 302 ♥

FIRE EXTINGUISHER KISS

Dress as a fireman and have a fire extinguisher conspic-
uously displayed. Explain it's because you plan to receive such
hot kisses they will need to be extinguished.

• 303 •

LOCK-UP KISS

Lock the two of you together with a padlock and chain.
Hide the key on yourself to be unlocked. Your love has to kiss
you 'til you are satisfied, then go looking for the key.
This is a great kiss for workaholics or if you haven't been
getting enough attention.

• 304 •

HALLOWEEN KISS

On Halloween, surprise your love by wearing a
costume, then ringing the door bell. When your love answers,
shout "Trick or Treat," then pucker your lips.

• 305 •

WHEELBARROW KISS

Turn your wheelbarrow into a chariot filled with pillows
and blankets. Wheel your love to a special place where you've
prepared a private picnic. Feed each other, kiss
and cuddle.

♥ 306 ♥

RECONCILE KISS

Hate reconciling your checking account? Make a
deal with your love to be kissed any way you want if the
checkbook is successfully balanced.

♥ 307 ♥

FINGER-POINTING KISS

Next time your love points a finger, grab it and kiss it.

♥ 308 ♥

CHERRY KISS

Start with a bowl of cherries. Feed the cherries to your
love and have him or her return the pits to you through a kiss.

♥ 309 ♥

BUTTERFLY KISS

Flutter your eyelashes in place of your lips to kiss your
love. Popular butterfly kiss locations are the cheeks, lips, ears
and eyes.

• 310 •

SPECIAL BOOK OF KISSES

Buy two of those pretty books with blank pages (most
book stores carry them). Once a month, bring the books out,
and together write loving messages in the other's book.
Of course, each loving thought is sealed with a kiss.

• 311 •

SIMPLE KISS

Give your love a lip-to-lip kiss, applying light pressure and a
little moisture.

• 312 •

HANDLE KISS

Take ahold of your love's ears and draw them in close for
a kiss.

• 313 •

PILLOW KISS

Share a pillow with your love tonight. Talk soft, and kiss lots.

• 314 •

FRENCH HUMMER KISS II

This is a deep kiss with humming sounds. Encourage
your love to hum along, too. People in earshot range aren't
going to know what's going on.

• 315 •

PROFILE KISS

Place a series of light kisses along the profile of
your love's face, beginning at the forehead. Conclude with a
prolonged kiss on the lips.

• 316 •

DOG KISS

Get up close to your love's face and generate short, quick
breaths through your nose to imitate a dog sniffing. Move your
nose around your love's face and neck the same way a
dog would.

♥ 317 ♥

SHOE KISSES

Surprise your love by putting candy kisses in the toes of his or her shoes.

♥ 318 ♥

KISS-FACE KISS

Shower your love's face with light kisses in quick succession.

♥ 319 ♥

LIMBO KISS

Beginning just under the chin, shower light kisses down the front of your love. This kiss is named after the game of limbo where the challenge is to see how low you can go.

♥ 320 ♥

FIRST-AID KISS

Next time your love has a hurt, cut, scrape, or bruise, play nurse, kissing the boo-boo.

♥ 321 ♥

STRIPPER KISS

Find the classic stripper tune "The Stripper" or hum
it, and come out stripping. Go as far as you want. End your
routine with sitting in your love's lap. Finish by a
big juicy kiss.

♥ 322 ♥

BOBBY-PIN KISS

Lock two bobby pins together to form "Xs." You now have a
great way to symbolize kisses. Clip sets of three onto
your love's pillow case, book or the lapel of a coat. It's a sweet
way to let your love know you're thinking of kissing him
or her even if you're not there at the moment.

♥ 323 ♥

CHEEKS KISS

Kiss your love on each cheek today. Make it twice on
each side.

• 324 •

PARISIAN KISS

Native Parisians greet one another with four alternating kisses
on the cheeks. Greet your love tonight with this kiss.
Then, keeping in the same spirit, French kiss your love. Vive
la France!

• 325 •

EAR WAX KISS

They say a good kiss puts a flush in your cheeks, but
a great kiss melts the wax in your ears. See for yourself with
your love tonight.

• 326 •

DRIVEWAY/PARKING SPACE KISS

You know how the police make a chalk outline of murder
victims? Have a friend make your outline (accentuating your
lips, of course) on your love's driveway or parking space.
Then chalk the words above your outline: "Don't have me
end up like this! Hurry inside and kiss me!"

♥ 327 ♥

TELEPHONE KISS

When your love picks up the phone, have a big red lip
shape stuck to the mouthpiece. *Idea: If you have more than one
phone, do it to all the phones in the house.*

♥ 328 ♥

STAMP KISS

Have a stamp made of your lips. That's right, put
your lip print on a piece of paper and take it to a stamp maker.
Have fun leaving messages for your love sealed with your
very own lips.

♥ 329 ♥

BUBBLE GUM KISS

Bring home bubble gum for you and your love to chew.
Each of you blows a bubble, then kisses one another. Guaranteed laughs.

⋆ 330 ⋆

ESCALATOR KISS
Next time you and your love ride an escalator,
the taller one should stand on the lower step, wrap your arms
around his or her neck and deliver a tender kiss.

⋆ 331 ⋆

LEFTOVERS KISSES
Have a bowl marked "leftovers" in the refrigerator.
When your love looks inside, have "leftover kisses" inside,
such as candy kisses, wax lips, "Xs" made out of pretzels,
pieces of cheese cut in the shape of your lips…your
imagination is the limit.

⋆ 332 ⋆

COFFEE CUP KISS
Bring your love his or her coffee in a mug you've
decorated with a red ribbon tied around the handle. Seize a
kiss before each sip.

• 333 •

THE LIFE SAVER GAME KISS
String a *Life Saver* candy onto a 12-inch piece of
string. Each of you take an end of the string in your mouth. A
drop of the hand begins the race to see which one of
you will get to the *Life Saver* first. The winner gets a kiss from
the loser. (Why not? You're there anyway.)

• 334 •

KISSING MONEY
Make your own kissing currency. Different kisses
have more value than others. You decide and pay your love
accordingly. Your love can cash them in for certain
chores. Remember, too many given out diminishes their
value.

• 335 •

BATHTUB KISS
Draw a bath for your love. Float a bottle filled with a love
note and chocolate kisses for your love to enjoy.

• 336 •

RING KISS

This kiss was made popular by couples when class rings
were exchanged. Hold the ring in front of your lips and kiss
your partner through the ring.

• 337 •

PILLOW TEST KISS

Similar to "The Princess and the Pea" test, this is the
"Your Love and the Head" test. Hide a chocolate kiss inside
your love's pillow, and see how long it takes to find it.
When it's found, tell your love he or she passed the love test
and that he or she really is your prince or princess.

• 338 •

HAIR BRUSHING KISS

Having your hair brushed in long, lingering strokes
by someone else feels fantastic. Talk your love into letting you
brush his or her hair. Finish with a kiss on the neck. *Idea:*
See if he or she will reciprocate.

▾ 339 ▾

KISSING TREE
The two of you find a special tree in your yard to have
as your very own kissing tree. Carve your initials into it, duck
behind it to steal kisses from each other, and, if possible,
climb up it. The two of you perch on a limb and make out like
a couple of love birds.

▾ 340 ▾

PEPPERONI KISS
Have a pepperoni pizza delivered to your house. When
placing the order, ask to have the pepperoni arranged in the
shape of lips or a big "X."

▾ 341 ▾

CASH IN KISSES
You know those little blue strips that come inside
the aluminum chocolate kiss wrappers? Well, declare them
redeemable for real kisses, and keep a bowl full of them
at all times.

• 342 •

NAPKIN KISS

Hide a chocolate kiss in your love's dinner napkin tonight.

• 343 •

MORNING GOODBYE KISS

Kiss your love sincerely this morning and tell him or her you
can't wait till you see him or her next.

• 344 •

COSTUME KISS

Rent costumes for the two of you. They could be a
sheik and a bellydancer, a doctor and a nurse, or Anthony and
Cleopatra. Assume the role and kiss like you think your
character would.

• 345 •

CONFETTI KISS

When next you see your love, throw a fist full of confetti into
the air and kiss before it all falls to the ground.

❤ 346 ❤

PLAY-DOH KISS

Make a lip shape out of *Play-Doh* and stick it some
place unexpected for your love to find (e.g: Under the lid of
the toilet seat, the bottom of a coffee cup, on the
TV remote).

❤ 347 ❤

SHOT KISS

Most people take a shot by throwing the head back
and taking one big swallow. Share a shot with your love by
taking the shot in your mouth and then, through a
kiss, sharing it.

❤ 348 ❤

TINGLE KISS

Remember your first kiss together when you had that
tingling sensation? Do it again by kissing each other's neck
and back.

♥ 349 ♥

SINGING KISS

Sit down and write out your favorite way to be kissed.
Now put your words to music using a song you already know,
or make up a melody. Find your love and try it out.
*Ideas: the more corny and off-key, the better. Make up choreography
to go with it.*

♥ 350 ♥

COPY KISS

Photocopy your lips and mail the copy to your love.

♥ 351 ♥

SHOW & KISS

A great kissing game. You show it, your love must kiss it.

♥ 352 ♥

ROLODEX KISS

Under "K" in your love's *Rolodex*, place a card that reads "For
kisses call…" with your phone number.

• 353 •

REPORT CARD KISS

A great idea if you'd like to improve your love's kissing.
Make a kissing report card out on your love. Grade on tender-
ness, hand movement, softness, lip position, tongue dexterity,
etc. Provide an opportunity to improve the grade.

• 354 •

REVOLVING DOOR KISS

The next time the two of you are confronted with a
revolving door, both of you squeeze into one section and
revolve around an extra turn while kissing.

• 355 •

AWARD KISS

Make a blue ribbon, trophy, or medal for "Best Kisser."
Tell your love he or she has made the finals, and tonight you
will be judging who's the winner.

♥ 356 ♥

CHAMPAGNE KISS

For no special reason bring home a bottle of champagne.
Toast your love under the bubbly and then seal it with a kiss.

♥ 357 ♥

EYEGLASS KISS

Locate your love's sunglasses or reading glasses. Plant
a lip print on each lens, then return them to your love to find.

♥ 358 ♥

KEEPSAKE KISS

Each of you press a lip print in the appropriately labeled box
provided as a memento.

♥ 359 ♥

ALERT KISS

Choose a noise device such as a bell, whistle, duck call,
trumpet or bugle. Sound your alarm whenever you want a kiss.
Only a kiss from your love can turn the noise off.

♥ 360 ♥

DIAPER KISS

Make an oversized diaper and pin it on the outside of your clothes. When your love is in sight, start jumping from one foot to the next saying, "I'll wet my pants if you don't hurry up and kiss me!"

♥ 361 ♥

SOMETHING'S-IN-MY-EYE KISS

Ask your love if he or she can see if there is something in your eye. When your love gazes in for a closer look, you zero in for a kiss.

♥ 362 ♥

BIKE KISS

Kiss your love while each of you are enjoying the outdoors pedaling around on your bikes. *Warning: this kiss requires impeccable timing and skill.*

• 363 •

COOKIE KISS

Give your love a box filled with kiss cookies. There
are three ways to do this: cut out cookies in the shape of lips;
cover your lips with frosting and kiss basic cookie
shapes; or decorate cookies with chocolate kisses. Or do all
three. Place in a beautiful box and send to your love.

• 364 •

POCKET KISS

Buy a bag of chocolate kisses. Go through your love's
closet and place a chocolate kiss in every pocket you can find.

• 365 •

365TH KISS

Take your pick. Pick out your favorite kiss from the first 364
and use it again here.

♥ 363 ♥

COOKIE KISS

Give your love a box filled with kiss cookies. There
are three ways to do this: cut out cookies in the shape of lips;
cover your lips with frosting and kiss basic cookie
shapes; or decorate cookies with chocolate kisses. Or do all
three. Place in a beautiful box and send to your love.

♥ 364 ♥

POCKET KISS

Buy a bag of chocolate kisses. Go through your love's
closet and place a chocolate kiss in every pocket you can find.

♥ 365 ♥

365TH KISS

Take your pick. Pick out your favorite kiss from the first 364
and use it again here.